REBUILDING TRUST

For Couples Committed to Recovery

About the booklet:

When a couple torn apart by sex addiction decides to mend their relationship, they will need tools to do so. This booklet is about those tools.

About the authors:

Jennifer P. Schneider, M.D., Ph.D., is a Fellow of the American College of Physicians and earned her doctorate in human genetics. She is the author of *Back from Betrayal: Recovering from His Affairs*. She writes and lectures on sexual addiction, coaddiction, and codependency.

Burt Schneider, M.A., M.Ed., is a former school administrator and broadcast journalist. He lectures with his wife. Both live in Arizona and have five children between them.

REBUILDING TRUST

For Couples Committed to Recovery

Jennifer P. Schneider
Burt Schneider

First published April, 1989.
Copyright (c) 1989, Hazelden Foundation.
All rights reserved. No portion of this publication
may be reproduced in any manner without the written
permission of the publisher.

ISBN: 0-89486-581-1
Library of Congress Catalog Card Number: 88-83916

Printed in the United States of America.

Editor's Note:
Hazelden Educational Materials offers a variety of information on chemical dependency and related areas. Our publications do not necessarily represent Hazelden or its programs, nor do they officially speak for any Twelve Step organization.

Contents

Introduction

Rebuilding a relationship is one of the biggest challenges facing couples recovering from sex addiction or coaddiction. As a couple several years into recovery from our own sex addiction and coaddiction, we often talk with others who are struggling with the challenges of recovering together at the same time as they are recovering individually. Because we would like to share with you what we have learned, we decided to write this booklet. Some of this material is mentioned in *Back from Betrayal: Recovering from His Affairs*, but in the year since the publication of that book we have learned about additional problems and issues.

Putting our thoughts down on paper has let us take another look at the issues we face daily in our own marriage. As we do in our individual recovery programs, we must also turn to a Power greater than ourselves in rebuilding trust and healing our relationship. Although we deal specifically with issues relating to sexual addiction and coaddiction, we hope our experience may also help those addicted to the bottle, other drugs, Lady Luck, work, or whatever has made life unmanageable.

This booklet is written at times from the perspective of the addict, at other times from the view of the coaddict, and often from the couple angle. This may require some shifts in your thinking as you read but is necessary since there are some issues that need to be resolved separately, while others must be dealt with together.

The stories we tell are all real, but we have changed names and details to protect people's privacy.

CHAPTER 1

Choosing to Recover

"Thank God," Susan said. "I think you and your wife can help me."

Susan had been trying to reach me all day. She left messages at work and at home. When I got to the office after several morning appointments, I returned her call.

I could hear the desperation in her voice. I had heard it before in talking with others about how the sexual issues in their relationships had become unmanageable.

Susan's story was familiar. She had spent the past two weeks following her husband's activities because of her sense that something was wrong. Despite his involvement in Alcoholics Anonymous and hers in Al-Anon, there was less serenity in their relationship than there had been in the four years since Mike stopped drinking.

"I never know what to expect from him. Sometimes he can be sweet and loving, but most of the time lately he goes off like a firecracker for no reason," she told me.

Susan confirmed what she had begun to suspect: Mike was involved with another woman. The pain she felt was mixed with confusion and fear. She somehow sensed that this was not the first time. She thought about the other times that Mike had acted strangely, the times when her Al-Anon friends had written off his behavior as a "dry drunk," the kind of behavior he used to show when drinking. Mike finally told Susan that indeed he was seeing someone else, a younger woman with whom he said he was in love. Susan's world fell in on her at that moment.

Over the next few weeks it became clear to Mike and Susan that even though Mike had been attending A.A. regularly and had not been drinking for four years, he had not in fact dealt with his compulsive nature. He now realized that instead of using alcohol to cover up his feelings, he was using sex. For the temporary relief he used to get from the bottle, he was now substituting the excitement of the chase and the conquest of a new woman, but he didn't feel very good about it. It was at the very A.A. meetings that had been his lifeline where he was now making connections with younger women still in their shaky, early days of recovery.

Mike didn't want his marriage to end, and he knew he would have to stop seeing the younger woman with whom he claimed he was in love. But at the same time, he couldn't envision life without the excitement of illicit romance. So much of his self-esteem was tied up in the validation he got from other women that he couldn't imagine stopping his affairs. Yet he realized he needed help. This latest affair was the third in a year.

When I spoke to him about a Twelve Step program for addiction to compulsive sexual behavior, rather than addiction to alcohol, he reacted strongly.

"They're not going to take this away too, are they?" he asked in a desperate tone.

Susan was proud of the way she had been able to let go of Mike's involvement with alcohol; she no longer looked for bottles in the old hiding places and had long ago ceased being a human breathalyzer or even wondering whether her husband had stopped at a bar on the way home.

Susan's sexual relationship with Mike was not ideal, but she thought it was typical of most couples. Mike was always the initiator in their lovemaking, and he wanted sex frequently. Because Susan didn't want to rock the boat, she never said no, regardless of how she felt that night. Deep down, she believed the way to keep Mike happy was to keep him satisfied sexually. She feared that if she didn't meet Mike's needs at home, he would seek sexual adventure elsewhere.

Susan did not realize that her attempts to control and manipulate Mike through sex were a symptom of her own sexual coaddiction. Nor did she realize that her fear of abandonment if she could not keep Mike sexually satisfied, and her belief that she indeed had the power to keep Mike from straying were also symptoms of sexual coaddiction. She, too, had not dealt with her underlying problem; like Mike, she had transferred the focus of her concern from alcohol to sex.

Both Mike and Susan needed and received help in order to begin their recovery process.

What Is Sexual Addiction?

Mike and Susan are a sexual addict and coaddict who have just hit bottom. Who are sex addicts? They are people whose sexual thinking and behavior causes problems in their lives, but who cannot control their actions despite their best efforts.

Sexual addicts are people whose lives are out of control because of their obsessive sexual thinking or compulsive sexual behavior or both. They continue harmful and dangerous practices despite consequences that would make a rational person stop. They use sex to deny feelings. Because we are all sexual persons, recovering from sexual addiction is especially difficult. For a sex addict, it's not just a matter of abstinence. Our sexuality is with us all the time.

Here are some examples of sex addicts:

- The husband who gets involved in yet another affair despite promises to himself and his wife not to have affairs.
- The unmarried woman who, by day, is a model kindergarten teacher but who, by night, frequents bars in order to find a stranger who will take her to bed—and cannot stop despite her fear of being injured or contracting AIDS.
- The college professor who has been warned that he will lose his job if he seduces one more student, yet does it anyway.
- The businessman who is arrested for soliciting an undercover policewoman posing as a prostitute, despite his arrest just six weeks earlier on the same charge.

- The out-of-work carpenter who spends half of his weekly unemployment check on pornography and at strip joints.
- The store manager who is fired because of complaints by female employees that he can't keep his hands to himself.
- The business executive who is unable to get her male employees to follow her directives because she has had a brief "fling" with each of them—and then wonders why she has difficulty having a professional relationship with them.
- The high school teacher who is sexual with her students.

The list could go on and on. We are a couple who have dealt with the problems of multiple affairs and have been recovering for five years. This booklet represents what we have learned in our own relationship and what other recovering couples have told us. For these other couples, the addict's compulsive behaviors included

- obsessive thinking about sex,
- affairs with people of the same or opposite sex,
- compulsive masturbation,
- excessive spending on pornography,
- patronizing prostitutes and massage parlors,
- anonymous sexual encounters in adult bookstores and parks, and
- exhibitionism and indecent telephone calls.

Often, there was more than one sexual behavior. This booklet does *not* deal with the legal and psychological problems of couples where one member has committed a criminal offense such as incest or rape.

What Is a Sexual Coaddict?*

The sexual coaddict is someone whose life is unmanageable because of his or her dependent relationship with a sex addict. Like spouses of alcoholics, sexual coaddicts often believe that

---

We'd like to thank Sandra Klein for the work she did in defining sexual coaddiction.

they are responsible for the addict's behavior and that they can control and change the addict. In their attempts to do this, they do things that prevent the addict from experiencing the consequences of his or her behavior. This is called *enabling*. They make the addiction easier for addicts to live with and postpone addicts' coming to terms with the fact that their lives are out of control and that they need help.

Coaddicts spend a lot of time obsessing about addicts' behavior and devising ways to control and manage them. They deny, cover up, make excuses, and, out of low self-esteem and fear of abandonment, are unable to confront the partner or get their own needs met. Their lack of success often results in frustration, anger, despair, and a sense of helplessness.

Here are some examples of sexual coaddicts:

- The wife who throws out her husband's pornography.
- The man who makes excuses for his wife's repeated affairs, telling himself it's his fault because the children are driving her crazy.
- The wife of the traveling salesman who makes love with her husband before every out-of-town trip to "prevent" him from being sexual with others.
- The man who doesn't let his wife know the pain and betrayal he's feeling because of her affairs.
- The pregnant wife who continues to have sex with her husband after catching gonorrhea from him, despite her fears of injuring her unborn child; she's afraid if she denies him sex he will be even more sexual with others.
- The woman who reluctantly accompanies her husband to swinging parties where they have sex with others, and tells herself that this way she can keep some control over the situation.
- The wife who tolerates her husband's anonymous sexual encounters with other men on the grounds that "at least it's not another woman."

Getting Help

Both members of the couple need to change if they are to develop a healthy relationship. If the coaddict is the first to recognize that life is unmanageable, he or she can begin to detach. Examples of detaching are

- paying less attention to the addict and more to his or her own needs and responsibilities,
- letting go of attempts to control the addict's life,
- letting the addict learn from the natural consequences of his or her behavior, and
- refusing to use encouragement, praise, or threats to manipulate.

In order to be able to begin detaching, the coaddict will probably need outside support, which can be found in Twelve Step fellowships and from counselors. The coaddict who detaches from the sex addict will often feel a sense of relief and enhanced self-confidence and energy. In detaching, the coaddict ceases to enable and provides a climate for change and recovery. The addict is likely to feel less and less comfortable acting out and will feel abandoned, threatened, and unloved.

Addicts often blame themselves and believe that they are the cause of the problems in the marriage. The fact is, both members of the couple need to change.

How Mike and Susan Got Help and How The Twelve Steps Work

Mike and Susan are at the beginning of the recovery process. As they change individually and in their interactions with each other, their marriage may or may not survive. At this early point, they already have two things going for them.

The most important is that they *both* recognize they need help. If Mike felt it is natural for a man to have affairs and his wife should accept this, it is very likely that, as Susan became healthier, she would decide to leave the relationship.

The second factor in Mike and Susan's favor is their A.A.

and Al-Anon experience. In these programs they became familiar with a model for recovery that has been successful for more than fifty years in helping alcoholics and their families recover. The core of these programs are the Twelve Steps, the first of which is an acknowledgment that the addict is powerless over the addiction and that family members, including the spouse, are powerless over the addict's behavior. The Second and Third Steps tell us that we do not have to deal with the problem alone — that we each have a Higher Power who is there to help if we are willing to ask for the help. Next, Steps Four and Five ask us to face our own weaknesses and to list our strengths — and to reveal these things about ourselves to our Higher Power and to another person, who may be a clergyperson, an A.A. sponsor, or a friend.

Many of us don't feel good about ourselves and have a great deal of guilt and shame about our behavior; we may believe "no one would like me if they knew what I was really like inside." The goal of the "confession" Step (Step Five), for addicts and coaddicts, is to demonstrate that other people will still consider us worthwhile people even if they know our shortcomings.

The next few Steps are concerned with being ready to have our Higher Power remove our character defects (Step Six); asking our Higher Power to remove those character defects (Step Seven); being willing to make amends to those we had harmed (Step Eight); and making amends wherever possible to those we have hurt (Step Nine). This includes making amends to ourselves.

The remainder of the program is a series of maintenance Steps, designed to help us remain in the new, healthier lifestyle we have chosen. These Steps include making an ongoing survey of our behavior and attitudes and righting wrongs whenever possible (Step Ten); praying and meditating in order to maintain the connection with our Higher Power (Step Eleven); and carrying the message of our recovery to others in need (Step Twelve).

Mike and Susan's familiarity with the Twelve Step program and their previous success in using it in recovery from alcoholism will make it much easier for them to apply the same principles to their sexual issues. Many others in Twelve Step programs for sexual addiction have had experience in A.A., Al-Anon, Overeaters Anonymous, Narcotics Anonymous, or other self-help, Twelve Step programs.

For members of these groups, in the course of the "searching and fearless moral inventory" of one's strengths and weaknesses that the Fourth Step calls for, evidence of compulsive sexual behavior or obsession with someone else's sexual behavior gets uncovered. Some people have found that working through the remaining Twelve Steps helps relieve their guilt and shame over those episodes. Others, however, have found that they cannot talk about their sexual past or current sexual behaviors at A.A. or Al-Anon meetings and need to be involved in specific recovery programs for sexual addiction and coaddiction.

"My A.A. sponsor just didn't understand my pain," Mike related. "He told me if I just concentrate on not drinking, everything would fall into place. But it didn't."

Twelve Step groups for sexual addiction and coaddiction are growing and are now active in many cities in the United States and in some other countries. You can write to the fellowships listed in the back of this booklet (Appendix B) for information about programs in your area. These organizations will usually be able to give you a telephone contact nearby. If there is no group in your area, you may be able to find a sympathetic A.A. or Al-Anon sponsor with whom you can talk about sexual problems. If not, we would advise you to find any Twelve Step meeting where you are welcome (because the program is fundamentally the same), and supplement going to meetings with telephone calls to other recovering people. When you meet other people in A.A. or Al-Anon who talk about sexual problems, you may then be able to start a meeting which deals with these concerns.

What a Commitment to Recovery Means

This booklet will specifically address the issues confronting a couple committed to traveling the path of recovery together. As recovering couples, we have a difficult task before us. We must each work on our individual recovery, and at the same time work on our relationship. It is an axiom among counselors that a relationship can be only as healthy as each person in it. At the beginning of the recovery process we typically have low self-esteem and tend to have overly dependent relationships. Our first priority must be our individual recovery; only when we have succeeded in improving our self-esteem will we be able to be in a relationship truly by choice and not out of dependency. Other books and booklets are available to assist you in your individual recovery. These are listed in the back (Appendix C).

Advantages of Recovery

Single people have the advantage of being able to focus on their own recovery needs without simultaneously trying to cope with the needs of another person. They also avoid the problems that come with attempting to break unhealthy patterns of relating to a partner and can look forward to making a fresh start in a new relationship. Couples who still love one another and decide to stay together are spared the turmoil of their family breaking up, the confusion and unhappiness of children whose parents are getting divorced, the financial and emotional costs of establishing separate households, and the fear of living alone.

Problems for the Coaddict

Couples face certain problems that a person recovering alone is spared. Probably the most difficult issue for coaddicts is dealing with the powerful negative feelings built up over the years. "How can I ever forgive my partner?" we ask ourselves as we again experience the feelings of betrayal and resentment because of our partner's affairs, hurtful behaviors, and emotional unavailability. Just because the compulsive sexual behavior has stopped, the pain and resentment don't disappear like magic. If we have been with our spouse for a long time, it may be that much harder to let go of the anger and resentment. For some, a residue of bitterness may always remain, no matter how committed we are to our recovery program.

The key to being able to let go of our resentment is to recognize that we are rarely innocent victims. We have to acknowledge some measure of responsibility for getting into the relationship, staying in it, and, most likely, "enabling" our spouses — that is, behaving in ways that protect them from experiencing the consequences of their behavior. Because of our efforts to please them, to be the perfect spouse, and to "make them happy," we may have inadvertently postponed the time when their life becomes so unmanageable that they seek help.

Through counseling, if available, and through our participation in Twelve Step programs, we may gradually heal ourselves and be more ready to heal our relationship.

A second major problem for the couple is related to the first. Alcoholics who work as bartenders and keep company with drinking friends would have a hard time staying sober no matter how committed they are to a Twelve Step program. Their sobriety would be safer if they were to change jobs and acquire some nondrinking friends. The married sexual coaddict in some ways is like the alcoholic bartender — we have the difficult task of overcoming our relationship addiction while continuing the relationship with the person to whom we have been addicted. These are different than the challenges faced by addicts. It is their responsibility to change their compulsive sexual behavior and thinking while interacting with, and having sexual relations with, the same person with whom they have for years participated in unhealthy patterns of relating.

Rebuilding Trust

Problems for the Addict

"The rest of my life may have been dull and boring, but I came alive when I was seeking new sexual adventures. I just don't know how I can survive without the affairs." This is a common reaction when addicts are confronted with stopping their sexual acting out.

As recovering addicts we had to learn a new way of living. The idea of life without our "drug" was pretty scary. Some of us became angry, depressed, and resentful. We railed against a society that didn't understand us. Others of us had to go back out there and experience some more pain before becoming willing to surrender this obsession with sex. Eventually, we realized that the changes we were making for ourselves were making our lives better. Still in the process, we needed the support of others who had gone before us in their own recovery programs. We learned about tools we could use to prevent relapse. We went to meetings, read the literature, talked on the telephone with other addicts, and asked for help from our Higher Power.

Problems for the Couple

Although there is some overlap in the timing, typical issues in early recovery include

- how to get help,
- choosing a counselor,
- celibacy periods,
- what to tell the spouse about the past,
- reestablishing trust,
- setting limits, and
- concentrating on one's own program.

Later, other relevant issues include

- what to tell the spouse about ongoing struggles,
- dealing with relapses and near-relapses,
- what to tell family members, friends, and business associates,

- how to talk with others without compromising our spouse's confidentiality,
- changes in the sexual relationship,
- control issues, and
- learning to enjoy life together.

In the chapters that follow, we will discuss these specific issues that couples must face as they recover individually and as a couple. Recovery as a couple may seem to be an overwhelming task. You may feel hopeless about the prospects of having a loving, caring relationship and recovering from compulsive behavior at the same time. You may be tempted to give up and isolate yourselves. Or you may think that things might be better with another person.

We believe that if a couple separates without dealing with problems in their marriage, both partners are likely to face similar problems in future relationships with others. For us, the authors, we have a history together, and we like the idea of starting over with the same person. And the faith and hope we have in the recovery process is strengthened as we meet other recovering couples who are willing to share what has worked for them.

CHAPTER 2

Early Recovery

For Couples: *How Do We Get Help?*

Change is frightening and uncomfortable; asking for help is difficult. As in the case of Mike and Susan, a crisis is often what prompts a decision to get help. If you are already involved in a Twelve Step program, you will probably want to talk with your sponsor or someone else in the program. They may refer you to Twelve Step programs for sexual addiction and coaddiction. Some chemical dependency treatment programs are also familiar with the concept of sexual addiction and can be a valuable resource in finding appropriate support groups.

If you have no prior A.A. or Al-Anon experience, you are most likely to seek out a counselor at the time of crisis. Many counselors know about compulsive sexual behavior and the self-help programs that deal with this problem. These counselors may be able to direct you to the appropriate group. Many cities have "Help on Call" or "Crisis Line" telephone numbers you can call and receive the listings of all self-help groups in your community. If you have been unable to locate an appropriate Twelve Step program in your community, write to the addresses in the back of this booklet (Appendix B) for information about the nearest group. Meetings of A.A. and Al-Anon that are open to the public are good places to start to learn about the Twelve Step approach to recovery. Later, starting a meeting of your own may also be appropriate.

For Couples: *How Do We Choose a Counselor?*

The best recovery path is probably a combination of a Twelve Step program and counseling. The counselor can

- let you know what to expect in various stages of your recovery,
- point out your enabling and addictive behaviors which arise from irrational thinking, and
- mediate and make suggestions when a couple's problems have proven difficult to resolve.

We believe that the core of the recovery program is the Twelve Step group. If you are unable to find a knowledgeable counselor, do not despair — many of us credit our recovery to our Twelve Step program without additional professional counseling.

It is important to find a counselor who is supportive of the Twelve Step program, and members of a self-help group are often an excellent source of information about knowledgeable counselors in your community. Going to a counselor who does not believe in self-help groups, and who will work against your Twelve Step program, rather than with it, is worse than going to no counselor at all.

What to Look for in a Counselor

When seeking treatment for *any* addiction, it is desirable to select a counselor who is knowledgeable about the addiction and who is interested in working along with its particular Twelve Step program. In the area of sexual addiction, however, additional matters should be clarified before deciding to work with a specific counselor.

Although most people in the helping professions choose the field because they truly care about people, many also get much of their own sense of self-worth from focusing on others rather than on themselves. Some counselors who choose to work in the area of sexuality are working through their own sexual issues. This may be okay, but before committing to work with a particular sex therapist, you need to learn about the person's credentials, experience, treatment approach, and biases. This is especially true because in most states sex therapists are not licensed; anyone can therefore claim to be an expert in this area. Choosing the wrong "expert" can do a lot of harm.

The counselor who said, "I gave myself permission to get as much sex as I wanted..."

Robert, a married thirty-five-year-old accountant, sought counseling because his multiple affairs were threatening his marriage. He chose a counselor who he'd heard had struggled with the same problem. The counselor told him, "Yes, I used to have affairs, but not anymore. I realized what my basic problem was — I just wasn't getting ENOUGH. So I gave myself permission to get as much sex as I wanted, and eventually I got tired of it. That's what I would recommend for you." It sounded too good to be true, and it was. Some months later, after several more affairs, Robert felt worse than ever about himself.

The counselor who failed to understand the client's lack of control...

Bill and Sylvia visited a sex therapist after Sylvia walked in on Bill as he was masturbating while making an obscene telephone call to a stranger. The therapist, having learned in his training that masturbation is healthy, told Bill to masturbate to thoughts of Sylvia instead of to the voice of a frightened stranger. Bill tried it, but found that once he began the activity he somehow always ended up on the phone. His therapist could not understand Bill's lack of control and Bill soon dropped out of counseling. The telephone calls eventually stopped only after he joined a self-help program that required abstinence from masturbation.

What Laura and Bruce didn't know about their counselor...

Laura and Bruce sought marriage counseling after Laura admitted to Bruce she'd had several affairs. Laura privately told the counselor she was still involved with another man, but didn't want Bruce to know this. The counselor believed that the way to deal with affairs was to work with the married couple on strengthening their relationship; the "other man" would then become less attractive and the affair would end. For several months, the counselor worked with Laura and Bruce on improving their communication; meanwhile, Laura's energy was focused on her extramarital relationship. Not surprisingly, the counseling did not improve things and eventually the couple stopped the therapy. What neither of them knew was that the counselor herself was involved in an extramarital affair, a fact that certainly biased her.

Unethical practice. . .

June, a slender, attractive forty-year-old former nurse, sought counseling after her husband, a physician, left her for a younger woman. She tearfully told her counselor that her husband had been her entire life, that she had pretended not to know about the many other women he'd been involved with, and that she just could not imagine life without him. The counselor assured her at each session that she was still a very desirable woman, and to prove it he had sex with her on several occasions. At first she was flattered by his attention, but eventually she ended the relationship, feeling confused and guilty.

Robert, Bill, Sylvia, Laura, Bruce, and June did not benefit from their counseling. In each case, treatment was influenced adversely by the counselor's own sexual beliefs and needs.

You have a right to question prospective counselors about their beliefs before committing to therapy. Here are some things you should consider during the first, get-acquainted appointment:

1. *If affairs or other compulsive sexual behaviors have been a problem for you, is the counselor familiar with the concept of sexual addiction?* Like the alcoholic who believes he or she can control drinking, Robert's counselor believed controlling sexual behavior was a matter of willpower; if he could do it, certainly his client could too. Bill's sex therapist,

knowing that masturbation is generally a healthy, normal activity, did not consider the possibility that it was actually triggering Bill's compulsive thinking and behavior.

Chemical dependency treatment programs have begun to recognize sexual addiction in some of their chemically dependent clients and are beginning to treat them for this problem. Chemical dependency treatment centers can be an excellent resource for the names of counselors knowledgeable about sexual addiction. Also, members of Twelve Step programs may know of counselors in the community who not only are aware of sexual addiction, but who consider the Twelve Steps a valuable recovery tool. Having worked with other people who have made the same journey, these counselors can pretty well predict how we will feel at each stage of our recovery. They can talk to us about our feelings of fear, loneliness, and loss. After all, years of obsessive thinking cannot be replaced overnight; there will be some hard times ahead. The counselor can also determine whether couple or individual counseling is best for us at any particular time, and when entry into a therapy group would be helpful.

2. *Is the counselor willing to work with a couple if one partner is concealing an affair from the other? How about if the affair is open but is still going on?* Laura and Bruce's counselor wanted to believe that it was possible to work on a couple's marriage while one person still was involved in an affair — after all, this is what the counselor herself was doing. This approach may occasionally succeed, but not frequently, and certainly *not* when the affair is part of a pattern. Most counselors and psychologists agree that one cannot counsel alcoholics who are still drinking; practicing alcoholics cannot think straight, and their drinking has a higher priority than anything else in their life. Similarly, people who are still focused on an affair cannot give their marriage the attention it deserves. Marriage counseling is not likely to be successful.

A concealed affair requires the counselor to collude with one spouse to deceive the other. Many counselors are justifiably uncomfortable being accomplices in deception.

   3. *Is the counselor male or female?* For other addictions, a counselor of either sex can be equally effective. But in the area of compulsive sexual behavior, the effect of the counselor's sex must be considered. Some recovering men who consulted a counselor prior to identifying themselves as sex addicts have advised us that they viewed their female counselors as sexual challenges. Instead of focusing on the therapy issues at hand, they tried to convince their counselors how emotionally healthy and how handsome they were.

Women who believe that sex is the most important sign of love, may also have difficulty with an opposite-sex counselor. Problems may be understated in an attempt to please and appear attractive to the counselor. In addition, the client may be especially vulnerable to sexual advances.

Sexual relations between therapists and clients do occur. In 1987 the *American Journal of Psychiatry* published a survey of over 1,400 psychiatrists who were members of the American Psychiatric Association (APA). When asked about their sexual experience with patients, more than 6 percent said they had sexual contact with their patients. Sexual relations between therapist and client are very detrimental to the client and to the therapeutic relationship. They are grounds for expulsion from the APA and, indeed, for loss of one's medical license.

If individual counseling is in order, we advise each member of a heterosexual couple initially to see a same-sex counselor if possible. (For a homosexual couple, there is not yet enough information to know what impact the sex of the counselor has on the effectiveness of treatment.)

For Couples: *Is a Celibacy Period for Us?*
How Celibacy Helps the Addict

An inpatient recovery program for sexual addiction that we, the authors, are familiar with requires a ninety day celibacy contract in which clients agree not to be sexual with oneself or others. The reasons the program gives are that maintaining celibacy

- prevents patients from using inappropriate sexual behavior to perpetuate the cycle of sexual dependency,
- lets patients view their spouse as a person instead of as a sex object, thus allowing them to experience intimacy without sex,
- helps patients become aware of their repressed feelings, and
- lets patients learn more effective ways of dealing with pain and guilt.

Sexual addicts in self-help programs have also found that a period of celibacy can be very useful especially in early recovery. To learn that we can survive without sex is a valuable lesson for those of us who have always believed that sex is our most important need. We learn to enjoy physical closeness for itself and begin to resolve problems in other ways than the shortcut in the bedroom.

For those of us who have used sex to suppress or numb our feelings, the idea of a celibacy period may not be welcome. We may think we'll explode or die without sex. We may go through a withdrawal similar to that experienced by alcoholics and other drug addicts. But we can find support if we talk with members of our support group as we challenge our belief that sex is our most important need.

If we are unable to stay with our original commitment of a month or two or three of abstinence, we need to take what we learned from this experience and perhaps make a decision with our partner to try again at another time. We must be gentle with ourselves as we learn to relate to our partner without being sexual.

Celibacy from the Coaddict's Point of View

Just as alcoholics who are sober learn that life is possible without the bottle, we can discover through a celibacy period that sex, in or out of marriage, is *optional*. There is a key difference, however, in these two situations. In an alcoholic marriage, the decision of the alcoholic to stop drinking does not force the spouse to do the same. The wife of the recovering alcoholic who chooses not to keep liquor in the house may have a drink at a friend's house or at a restaurant. In contrast, if one member of a couple decides to give up sex, the spouse is automatically denied sexual intimacy.

The problem with one-sided celibacy decisions, made by the addict, is that they perpetuate the pattern we lived in before recovery. As coaddicts, many of us spent years putting our spouse's needs ahead of ours, especially their sexual needs. We may never have said no to their sexual wishes, reasoning that if they got enough sex at home they would be less likely to stray. If, in early recovery, they decide to be celibate, we may feel nothing has changed — that our sexual needs are still being ignored. The result is likely to be resentment, followed by guilt at our unwillingness to do whatever it takes to help them succeed.

Coaddicts may also feel rejected and unwanted. For many of us, one of our core beliefs is that sex is the most important sign of love. If our spouses tell us they want to be abstinent for a while, we might conclude they no longer love us. If we give in to an impulse to try to seduce them, we will be sabotaging their recovery program. Caught between our needs and theirs, we are likely to feel insecure and resentful.

Sex in a marriage is a relationship issue. To feel comfortable about a period of celibacy, both spouses must be involved in the decision. During a mutually agreed on abstinence period, we may discover that our spouse wants us for more than just our body, and that we can get love without giving sex. When they continue to act lovingly toward us, we learn that our belief that sex is the most important sign of love is irrational. We realize that we are worthwhile people, that we are lovable for ourselves, and that sex is *not* the most important sign of love.

As coaddicts who have tried to control our spouse through sex, a period of abstinence forces us to adopt new coping strategies and face problems directly. Instead of using sex as a solution, we learn to talk about problems and try to solve them constructively.

Many of us have spent years trying to be the perfect sexual partner while sublimating our own needs. We may have felt guilty saying no, no matter what our mood. A celibacy period disrupts this unhealthy pattern and allows us to begin to pay attention to our own needs.

In early recovery, we often feel so much anger and resentment against our spouse that we need a cooling-off period. We may simply not want any physical intimacy for a time, and a celibacy agreement allows us to have this interval without feeling guilty about it.

Celibacy for Both the Addict and Coaddict

As couples, we may have never learned how to relate intimately in a nonsexual way. During an abstinence period we have an opportunity to explore new pathways — to touch each other without the touching being a prelude to sex, to spend time together talking, to pay attention to each other, to rekindle romance.

Many couples have little experience with nonsexual touching, and a counselor can be very helpful in bringing this into a relationship. We suggest having each person prepare a list of behaviors they would like to do or experience — she might enjoy having him touch her shoulder when he walks by. He might like holding her hand at the movies. She may want to give him a hug when she arrives home from work. A counselor can help with specific suggestions.

A celibacy period is not for all couples. For those who are considering it, it is essential that the decision be made jointly, after discussion of the reasons. We should not use abstinence to punish our partner, nor to avoid dealing with marriage problems, nor as a way to avoid intimacy. But for many couples in early recovery, a temporary celibacy period can be a time of spiritual growth and increased intimacy.

For Couples: *How Do We Rebuild Trust in Each Other?*

If our spouse has had sexual affairs with other men or women, we may have felt that we can never trust our partner again. At the same time, we recognize that without trust we cannot put our relationship back together. This is a real dilemma for those of us who want to save our marriage.

Trust in another person involves predictability, dependability, and faith. People who are predictable will behave the same way in the future as they have in the past. Dependable people are those who can be relied on. Both predictability and dependability reflect past behavior. But since future behavior does not always mirror the past, faith is our belief, based on our partners' past behavior, that they will continue to be responsive and caring, and that they will not hurt us emotionally.

When we learn of our partners' affairs, all the elements of trust vanish. We discover their past behavior has been very different from what we were led to believe, and we therefore have no basis from which to predict their future behavior. We no longer feel we can depend on their concern for us. Moreover, not only can we no longer be certain of the consistency of their attitudes, we now realize we don't even *know* what their attitudes are.

Rebuilding trust is the major task for couples after an affair is revealed. This process takes months to years and requires much work on the part of both partners. Honesty, predictability, and dependability are the key elements both spouses must consistently show for the relationship to heal. Involvement in a recovery program encourages this process.

How the Addict Can Rebuild a Damaged Relationship

As addicts, we need to show a willingness to answer questions about our past, even if it is uncomfortable for us to do so. We need to show our spouse consistency in our behavior to contrast with our history of lies and inconsistencies. And we need to be committed to our self-help program.

In addition to consistently honest behavior, we need to show our spouse a consistently *caring* attitude. This will also contribute to restoring trust in the damaged relationship. It is helpful to acknowledge the lack of trust and to make special efforts to be honest in all our activities. For example, we may find it useful to telephone if plans change, and to follow through on commitments. Over time, fewer reassurances will be needed.

Another important element is open communication. Prior to recovery, we frequently didn't tell our partner what was going on in our head. This added to their sense of insecurity and distrust. When we share our doubts, our successes and failures, and our feelings, we are likely to feel closer to and more trusting of each other. For those of us who have covered up our feelings for most of our lives, this can be a monumental task, but it is essential for restoration of trust and for the survival of the relationship.

Since rebuilding trust takes time, a period of stress and distrust is unavoidable. We cannot expect forgiveness overnight. Each day of honest, consistent, and trustworthy behavior builds upon the previous day, until a foundation exists on which new trust can be based.

For the Addict: *How Much Should I Tell My Spouse about My Past Behaviors?*

When we were having affairs, visiting prostitutes or pornographic bookstores, or spending our time and emotional energy in other compulsive sexual behaviors, our partner often suspected it. And when evidence of the latest affair or other behavior was so blatant that we could no longer deny it, a crisis occurred in our marriage. Our spouses asked us for more information. We may have lied to them then. Now, to rebuild trust, we must decide how much to reveal about our past.

One program for sexual addicts cautions its members, especially those in early recovery, against confessing past sexual activities to the spouse. Members suggest that newcomers not discuss their sexual past with their spouse or children until spending some time in the program. Even then, they suggest an addict's sponsor and his or her recovery group should be consulted first.

*Hope and Recovery: A Twelve-Step Guide for Healing from Compulsive Sexual Behavior** expresses the same point of view. The authors of this book advise waiting to tell the spouse until the addict has discussed it with the group, prayed about it, and felt it was the right time to do so. They advise planning in advance exactly what to tell the partner and having your sponsor present at that time.

If affairs or the preoccupation with others has been a recurring theme in your marriage, however, it may be advisable to give your partner some information. Some of us have found that our willingness to answer questions was a critical element in restoring trust in the relationship. Our partners lived through years of our mood swings and their obsessive attempts to understand them, explain them, and control us; they chose to believe our statements that nothing unusual was going on, although their gut was telling them the opposite; many spouses began to think they were crazy. Hearing the truth from us provides validation for their "crazy" feelings and confirms their sanity, as well as explains the many puzzling situations they may not have understood. After months or years of our lying, our willingness to tell the truth is a beginning in the long process of rebuilding trust.

In addictive relationships, things are usually out of balance. One partner often has the power to make the other happy and to make most decisions that affect the relationship. When only one person in the relationship decides what information the other should have about the past, we perpetuate the belief that

---

*Hope and Recovery: A Twelve Step Guide for Healing from Compulsive Sexual Behavior (Minneapolis: CompCare, 1987).

we are better judges of what is best for our partners than they are themselves. This is rarely the case. Many spouses are relieved to have the information. We must trust that they are able to make appropriate decisions about how much they need to know. Our answers validate their sanity, let them understand why things happened when they did, and confirm that their gut feelings were rooted in reality.

Some spouses, however, may prefer to have a minimum of information. One member of a support group told other members: "My wife had an affair with one of my best friends and then told me every little detail about it. I spent months obsessing about him and her. Whenever I heard his name I got sick to my stomach. Every time I met someone who even looked like him, I wanted to kill him. When she had another affair, she didn't tell me his name. I don't know who it was, and I don't want to know. If she needs to talk about it with someone, she can tell her support group. I don't need to beat myself up any more."

Some spouses need certain details about our past in order to sort out in their minds the craziness they went through. Some of them need the secrets out in the open in order to make a fresh start. Others believe it is in their best interest not to have more than the barest of facts; they recognize they would use detailed information to try to control our behavior and to make themselves feel worse. They may want to know only that the affairs, the visits to pornographic bookstores, or our other compulsive sexual behavior has stopped and that we are getting help to prevent a relapse. They may want to know only that we are committed to our marriage. We have found that most people usually do not ask for information they are not ready to hear.

If our relationship is to heal, we must treat each other with honesty and respect. Respect means letting our partner decide how much they need to know and then answering their questions thoughtfully.

Each situation is different, and each must be decided individually; there are no universal answers.

For the Coaddict: *How Do I Avoid Monitoring My Spouse's Recovery Program?*

Sharon and Pete recently joined self-help groups for Sharon's promiscuity and Pete's reaction to it. Pete reported to his therapist, "Sharon's no longer sleeping around, but I get afraid whenever she misses a meeting. Also, I find myself trying harder than ever to keep things perfect at home. I know it's been difficult for her to give up her behavior, so I don't want to do anything that might make her go back out there. My Twelve Step sponsor says I'm still trying to control her. I *know* I'm powerless over her, but I just can't help worrying. I'm feeling very discouraged."

Sharon says, "Pete thinks *I'm* the one with the problem, but you should hear him ordering the kids around like a general. No wonder they can never make any decisions on their own! I don't know what he's learning at those meetings he goes to, but I don't think it's rubbed off yet on his behavior. He still grills me about where I've been, especially on meeting nights."

Sharon and Pete are behaving exactly as expected for their stage of recovery. Pete by now understands intellectually that his behavior is controlling, but old habits die hard, and understanding is often difficult to translate into action. Pete has acknowledged there is a problem but has not changed his behavior. He will find that, with time, there will be more occasions when he is able to stop himself from quizzing Sharon or when he is willing to risk her displeasure without experiencing the panic of imminent abandonment. The recovery program teaches us to believe in "progress, not perfection." Progress may seem very slow at first, and monitoring our spouse's recovery is inevitable in the beginning. We need to gauge our progress by the times we succeed, not by the times we fail.

As for Sharon, having felt guilty and blameworthy all these years, she has now learned to recognize that Pete, too, contributed to the problems in the relationship. His controlling behavior with their children is much clearer to her than to him, as he is still very focused on his wife. Pointing out his faults, referred to in self-help meetings as "taking his inventory," is not only unavoidable, but at times she positively enjoys it. This, too, is to be expected.

For the Addict: *How Do I Take Responsibility for My Program?*

A definite pitfall to avoid in early recovery is the tendency to use your spouse to police your recovery. Beth, a thirty-six-year-old teacher, reported shortly after she and her husband began their recovery, "Larry told me he can't trust himself yet with extra money. He wants me to help him stay out of the pornographic bookstores by giving him only enough money to get through the day and asking him to account for every penny spent."

The problem with this arrangement is that it allows Larry to avoid responsibility for his recovery and casts Beth in the parental role in their relationship. Sooner or later Larry will begin to resent Beth's role as police officer. He may respond by interacting negatively with her or by becoming the rebellious little boy who is going to "show Mommy" by acting out.

Furthermore, this arrangement perpetuates Beth's belief that she can control her husband's behavior. We need to focus on our recovery and let our spouses focus on their recovery. If we cannot trust ourselves with extra money, we need to make a plan to feel safe that does not include supervision by our spouse.

In our recovery, we want to "get" the program immediately, to find the answers as soon as possible so we can get on with our life. But we must be gentle with ourselves. Recovery is a one-day-at-a-time process. Early on, we need to make every effort to focus on our recovery, not our spouse's, but we shouldn't feel like failures if we occasionally find ourselves looking over the shoulder of our partner.

For the Coaddict: *What Is a Limit and What Is an Ultimatum?*

" 'If you ever have another affair, I'm leaving you' — that's what I told my wife a dozen times," says a male hospital orderly, thirty-six years old. "Well, she did, and I didn't. Now that we're both in a Twelve Step program and are seeing a counselor, I'm feeling better about myself, and one of the things I know is that I just don't want to go through the pain of another affair. If she has another one, I really *will* leave, but what's the point of my saying anything to her? It will sound like another one of those empty threats I never followed through on."

In the past we were so fearful of abandonment that, rather than risk confronting our partners, we were willing to tolerate behaviors that hurt us. There were always exceptions and special circumstances we used to explain and excuse their behavior. There was always a reason, however implausible, we told ourselves to avoid facing the truth. We had no clear boundaries. We depended on others to tell us how we felt, what we thought, and how much we were worth. Decisions were based on what we thought our spouse wanted, not on what we wanted.

A major goal in recovery is to improve our self-esteem, so we are willing to pay attention to our needs and feelings, rather than to focus on others. At times, being assertive means risking another person's displeasure. We will be able to risk this only when we cease to believe that our partner is essential to our survival.

As our self-esteem improves, we no longer believe in keeping our spouse at any cost. When the possibility of living alone ceases to feel like a fate worse than death, we are ready to consider what is or is not acceptable to us in our relationship. This is the point at which we may begin to entertain the possibility of leaving if our spouse is unwilling to be faithful.

We will eventually have enough self-esteem to develop some limits or boundaries for the relationship. Sometimes the limits are discussed by the couple, along with the consequences if the limits are broken. In other marriages, for example, a spouse may know the limits but has not discussed them with his or her partner.

Many of us have confused establishing limits with giving an ultimatum. We may have threatened to leave our spouses if they again had sex with others, but we did not follow through. Or if we did leave, we soon found we couldn't be happy without them and took them back. We used threats to try to control their behavior.

Setting a limit differs from making a threat. Rather than trying to control another person, we are letting him or her know which behaviors are acceptable to us and which aren't. Our spouse can choose how to behave, and we can choose whether or not to live with that behavior. For one man who has decided that living alone is preferable to living with a wife who has affairs, another affair is his limit. His wife understands that if she chooses to have another affair, her marriage will end.

A man who is in a recovery program still has occasional "slips" consisting of anonymous sex with other men. His wife, hopeful that her husband's relapses will eventually stop, wants to stay in the marriage with him because she sees progress. However, she does not want to risk catching AIDS, herpes, or other sexually transmitted diseases. For her own protection, she has decided she cannot have sexual relations with him as long as he continues to have sex with others.

For some, the limit may be the spouse's affair or visiting a prostitute. For others, it is not some particular sexual behavior but, rather, evidence that there is no longer a commitment to working on recovery. No longer attending meetings may be a prelude to resumption of the compulsive behavior. Some spouses might choose to separate at this point, even before a "slip" actually occurs.

At the beginning of our own recovery we may be reluctant to set limits in our marriage. In the past we may have made frequent threats and never followed through. We may be fearful of being judged if we appear to be judging our partner. Some of us, aware that our own boundaries have been blurred for so long, feel we are in no position to define limits for anyone else's behavior. As we progress in our own recovery and as our own relapses become less frequent, we will most likely feel more comfortable about building expectations and accountability into our relationship.

As recovering spouses, we need to learn about establishing boundaries for our own behavior as well. In the past, out of fear that our partner would leave us, we may have engaged in behaviors with which we were uncomfortable. As our self-esteem improves, we are able to risk saying no. We might say no to a particular sexual activity that we never liked. Or we might tell our recovering partners we don't want to hear about their latest struggle with their obsession. Whatever it is, learning to say no, to establish boundaries for ourselves, is a part of the new self-respect we are acquiring.

For the Coaddict: *Sexually Transmitted Diseases*

In recent years, sexually transmitted diseases (STDs) have been on the mind of nearly every sexually active person. Even couples who have been mutually monogamous for years worry about the possibility of contracting Acquired Immune Deficiency Syndrome (AIDS), a fatal disease which is having more impact on the country's sexual practices than all the lectures on morality ever did. (Celibacy and mutual monogamy are the only guaranteed ways to avoid sexual transmission of AIDS, herpes, and other STDs).

A prominent physician said on a television program, "When you have sex with someone, you're also having sex with everyone he or she had sex with in the past five years." This is a sobering thought for those of us whose spouse engaged in extramarital sexual activity. In the past, what we risked by continuing to have sex with our spouse was the possibility of acquiring a bacterial disease, such as syphilis or gonorrhea, which is easily treated with antibiotics; or at worst, a case of herpes which might recur for years. But now, with the AIDS epidemic, we are risking our very lives and those of our unborn children.

If the fear of abandonment is so overwhelming that we cannot refuse sex to our spouses who are sexually active with others, then at least we must insist on the use of condoms 100 percent of the time. We must not become complacent if they produce a negative AIDS blood test; all this tells us is that they were probably not infected when they had the test. (There is still a small chance that they are infected, as the AIDS test does not turn positive for about six weeks after infection.) The negative test is no guarantee about today or tomorrow if our spouse is continuing extramarital sex.

For the Addict: *Sexually Transmitted Diseases*

Acknowledging our powerlessness over our compulsive sexual behavior does not relieve us of responsibility for our own health and our partner's. If we had sexual contact with others, we need to be honest and tell our partner so he or she can make an informed choice about whether to continue to be sexual with us. If our partner chooses to abstain from sex with us, we must not then use this as an excuse for further sexual acting out. Rather, we need to intensify our involvement in our recovery program so that, when it is safe, we can, if our partner agrees, resume sexual relations with our partner.

CHAPTER 3

Ongoing Recovery

*"If he would only stop the affairs (or the visits to
prostitutes, or the compulsive masturbation, or. . .)
then our marriage would be fine, and we could then
work out all our other problems."*

This is the illusion that many of us have had about our
partner's compulsive sexual behavior. One of the unhappy facts
those in recovery quickly learn is that the problems don't stop
when the behavior ceases. True, the problems are *different*, but
they may be just as serious. It can be very demoralizing to hear
about the end of a marriage between two people who have
been recovering in Twelve Step programs. Unfortunately, this
is quite common. In addition to all the usual stresses of any
marriage, recovering couples have to deal with other predictable
problems related to their addictions and codependency.
Cessation of the compulsive behavior is only the beginning
of the recovery process.

In his book, *Stage II Recovery,* Earnie Larsen defines Stage I
Recovery as breaking the addiction, and Stage II Recovery as
learning to make relationships work. In this chapter we will
discuss some of the issues couples face who have survived the
first hurdle: they have initiated some changes and have
committed themselves to attending self-help programs. They
may also have sought professional counseling. They have
affirmed to each other their intention to stay together. Some
of them may eventually decide to separate, but in this chapter
we will assume that for each of our readers, saving the marriage
is a high priority.

For Couples: *How Will We Ever Resolve Our Control Issues?*

Before recovery, the addict's behavior so dominated the thinking of both people in the relationship that neither was fully aware of other real problems in the family. When the major problem in a couple's relationship ceases to be sexual behavior, it is often replaced by a tendency to try to control other people's behavior in order to achieve their own goals. Several couples in ongoing recovery have told us that control is now the major problem in their marriage. This problem has its roots in our childhood.

Many of us came from unhealthy families, families in which our childhood needs for nurturing were not entirely met. Long before we could be specifically identified as addicts or coaddicts, we learned coping strategies that turned us into codependents, people of low self-esteem who look to others for approval and validation of self-worth. Many of us spent our childhoods trying to understand and make sense of the ever-changing or even chaotic world in which we lived. Having felt helpless and powerless in our early years, many of us try as adults to control and manipulate our environment in order to avoid feeling helpless again.

Before recovery, the addict's energies were focused on trying to control the compulsive behavior; the spouse's efforts were directed at controlling the addict and the environment. During recovery, both of us may find ourselves trying to control everything around us. Add to this an increased awareness of the nature of controlling behavior, and you have a recipe for conflict.

Conflict: Dealing with Our Children's Problems

In our own household, Burt took care of much of the day-to-day routine. Living with five teenagers was not easy and Burt found himself trying to control much of what was impossible to control. Since he no longer used his old self-destructive ways of dealing with stress, he concentrated on making sure everything was in place in the home, that all attended meals on time, and that I was ready to be congenial with him despite my exhaustion at the end of a busy day of seeing patients and making hospital rounds. Because he had unrealistic expectations of how things should be, Burt felt resentful and was setting himself up for a slip.

Children are often the focus of parents' struggle for control. Because addiction can often be traced from one generation to the next, it is not uncommon for teenage children of a recovering couple to be having their own struggles with addictive behavior. They may already be entrenched in one of several roles children often assume in such families, and may either be overly responsible or perpetually in trouble.

In addition to dealing with their own children's codependency, the couple may also have to struggle with a child's involvement with alcohol and other drugs. The mother and father may each have definite but conflicting ideas on how to best help the child. Al-Anon teaches us to "let go with love," which means acknowledging that we cannot control other people, and that no matter how much we love them and how clearly we can anticipate the negative consequences, we must let them make their own mistakes. When our children are involved, this is easier said than done.

Conflict: Controlling Behavior between Husband and Wife Converts Them into a Parent-Child Relationship

Many of us have also found ourselves overreacting to some minor problem with our spouse only to realize later that inside we were feeling like a little child arguing with Mom or Dad. For those of us who have not yet sorted through our feelings about our childhood, any controlling behavior by our partner is likely to cast him or her—in our mind—in the role of a parent. We may then feel and act like a rebellious child. Conflict is likely to escalate and solving problems is likely to be difficult.

Many spouses of recovering addicts have found that they must make a special effort to avoid behavior that could be interpreted by the addict as attempts to control. Give advice, offer a helpful suggestion, and you may find yourself the target of the addict's unresolved anger toward his or her parents. This common problem points out that there can be no recovery for couples unless there is first individual recovery; until there is some resolution of childhood issues like this one, it will be difficult to relate consistently to our partner as an adult.

Resolving the Conflicts

Although there are no easy answers to conflicts over control, help is available in Steps Ten and Eleven of the Twelve Step program. We can take an ongoing personal inventory and admit when we are wrong. We can continue our spiritual program of prayer and meditation, asking for knowledge of our Higher Power's will for us and the power to carry it out. We must recognize that progress is slow and that lifelong coping habits don't change overnight. We need to be gentle with ourselves when we recognize we are wrong. As the program tells us, we strive for progress, not perfection.

If feelings become so negative that calm discussion seems impossible, a third person may be helpful for resolving conflict. This may be a program sponsor, a counselor, or a clergyperson. We need to avoid "dumping" on a friend; it is more helpful to spend an hour at a Twelve Step meeting than to spend an hour complaining to a friend about our spouse's unreasonable behavior.

We have personally found two very helpful ways of airing our feelings at times when a back-and-forth discussion is likely to turn into an argument.

The first is letter writing. In a letter to our partner, we state our feelings about the situation. We use "I" messages ("I felt angry when you said...because...") and we avoid insults. The time it takes to write a letter allows us to cool down and avoid saying things we may regret later. Letter writing gives us the time we need to state our case without reacting to the facial expressions and body language of our partner. Letters give us time for reflection and the opportunity to forgive and forget. Our partner then has the opportunity to read the letter, reflect on it, and write a response or take action.

A second technique we use is silent listening. When

something is really bothering one of us, we find it helpful to announce to the other that we want to be heard without interruption. No matter how long it takes to say everything one of us wants to say, the other cannot say a word, no matter how much the other disagrees with, or wants to explain, or has an answer for what has been said. When the first person is finished, then the other has as much time as is needed to respond. Sometimes a second round of talking is necessary before both of us have said everything we want to say.

The problem with attempting to have a discussion when feelings are strong is that the speaker often does not even get to finish a sentence before the partner is ready with a heated rebuttal or an explanation. Each person may be more interested in thinking of a reply than in listening to what the other is saying. The advantage of the "no interruption" rule is that the speaker does not have to rush to get out a thought before being interrupted, and the listener can pay attention to the partner rather than immediately responding. As in the letter writing technique, it is most helpful if the speaker can avoid insults and phrase his or her words in "I" messages, instead of "you" messages, as much as possible.

If you have never tried either of these techniques, we advise the letter-writing first. After you've had some experience in stating your feelings when you're alone, you can then try the face-to-face uninterrupted speaking technique. With practice, both of these methods can help get your relationship back on track when it has been derailed by feelings of resentment and anger.

One important point to remember: There are some issues upon which you may never agree; it is okay to agree to disagree.

For the Addict: *How Much Should I Tell My Spouse about My Present Struggles?*

For some of us, the compulsion to be sexual in destructive ways was lifted when we got into the program. For others, it is an ongoing struggle. Recovering persons frequently wonder how much to share with their spouses about their struggles, their near-slips, and their relapses. If a man has a one-night stand after two years of monogamy, should he tell his wife? What if he broke his own rule and went into a pornographic bookstore — but managed to leave before he connected with another person: does she need to know that? What if she spent all day fantasizing about a man she talked to briefly? Should she tell her husband about it?

Earlier, we discussed what to tell our spouse about sexual activities that *preceded* entry into recovery; this is a different issue from sharing struggles that occur *during* recovery. Deciding what to tell our spouse is difficult because it bears on issues of honesty, trust, control, limit setting, accepting responsibility for one's own program, and concern for our spouse's feelings. What is right for one couple may not be right for another. Here are some different perspectives on this problem:

"I only want to know if she's planning to break
the agreement we made — no more affairs. . ."

"Early in my own recovery I wanted to know everything she was thinking. I can see now that I was feeling that if I knew what was going on in her mind then I could at least be prepared for the worst. I had a doomsday mentality then and no trust in the program — neither hers nor mine. It helped me to feel in control, to know exactly where she was in her program. Of course, whenever she told me she'd been very attracted to another man I felt terrible. It was like being rejected all over again. But it felt even worse *not to know,* so I kept asking. Now that I'm healthier, I realize that I really don't want to know all that stuff; I would still feel bad hearing it, and knowing wouldn't serve any purpose. I want to know only if she's planning to break the agreement we have — no more affairs — or if she's going through some terrible struggle that is clearly affecting our relationship. She can discuss everything else with her group rather than with me." (man, forty-five)

*"My husband was already in a recovery program
when I met him..."*

"We decided there would be no secrets between us, so at first we went over everything in great detail — all his thoughts as well as his actions. It wasn't easy for me! Now, if he's having problems, it's enough for him to tell me, 'I'm having a rough day with my urges.' I don't need to know all the gory details. I just want to know if he's having a difficult time." (woman, thirty)

"Clear the air right away..."

"My husband always tells me when he has a slip. It's not that I insist on knowing, but he acts so dejected and guilty around me that it's better for us to clear the air right away and get on with our lives. Actually I feel very encouraged. He's so obviously committed to the program, and his slips are happening less and less frequently, and he's so much more open with me and willing to talk that it gets easier and easier to deal with the slips." (woman, thirty-five)

"No secrets..."

"It's very important in our recovery together that we have no secrets between us. Every small secret is a brick which could build a wall between us. We've both agreed that we need to talk about everything, even if it's painful." (man, twenty-eight)

"Instead, I talked about it with my group..."

"Our relationship is pretty strained right now. Recently I went to a massage parlor just for a massage but ended up getting 'the works.' I resolved to tell her, but hearing about another relapse would only discourage her more and strain our relationship further. Instead, I talked about it with my group and worked out strategies for avoiding going into the massage parlor in the first place. I think that not telling her was the right decision for us." (man, fifty)

Rebuilding Trust

> *"It's better if she talks about it... not to me..."*

"For a while my wife was confusing pain and progress. She let me see all the pain so I would think she was making progress. It was really dumping on me. I, in turn, was not honest in telling her my reactions. I was hurt, and I didn't really want to hear what she was telling, but I thought I had to be supportive. It's better if she talks about it to her group and not to me." (man, thirty-nine)

Establishing Guidelines

The ideal solution to this complex issue is to talk with each other about it and come up with guidelines before we need them.

As coaddicts, we can ask ourselves *why* we want to know whatever it is we want to know.

- Is it in order to get a feeling of control over the situation?
- Is it to maintain honesty in the relationship?
- Is it to better understand our spouse's behavior?
- Is it out of fear of catching a sexually transmitted disease?
- Is it because we have decided we would prefer living alone to coping with affairs?

As addicts we can ask ourselves *why* we want to tell our spouses.

- Is it to get absolution from him or her?
- Is it to feel as though I'm getting a fresh start?
- Is it because we've agreed with each other to be honest?
- Is it because I believe it will help our relationship if he or she knows what's happening in my psyche?
- Is it because I want his or her help in a difficult time?
- Is it because I'm afraid I might infect him or her with a disease?

Or we can ask ourselves why we *don't* want to tell our partners.

- Is it to spare his or her feelings?
- Is it because the two of us have decided that he or she doesn't want to hear about it?
- Is it because we've agreed to discuss only a relapse, not just obsessive thinking?
- Is it because I don't think our relationship could survive another slip?
- Is it because I know he or she will leave me?
- Is it because not telling gives me the option of doing it again?
- Is it because I'm too ashamed and don't want him or her to think badly of me?
- Is it because I've already discussed it in my group and have taken steps to decrease the likelihood of another relapse?

If we can't make a decision together as a couple, we will each need to work out alone what is best. It is tempting to take the easier, softer way and avoid discussing painful matters with our partner. But the Twelve Step program is a program of rigorous honesty. This does not mean "dumping" everything on our spouse, but it does mean looking honestly at our motives.

For the Coaddict: *How Do I Deal with My Spouse's Near-Relapses and Relapses?*

What happens when our spouse is acting as crazy as in the bad old days, even though he or she still seems as committed to the program as we are? What do we do when we are convinced our spouse is headed for a relapse?

The program tells us that we did not cause the problem and we cannot cure it. Prior to embarking on our own recovery, our immediate response to a change in their behavior was to *do something.* We believed erroneously that we not only had the power to make them change, but that we also had the responsibility to put that power to good use. Typically, we would consult our closest friend, map out a strategy, and immediately begin to put it into effect. If their behavior seemed suspicious, we would ask ourselves, *What did I do wrong, and what changes can I make to improve things?* as though the situation were our responsibility.

Some of us increased our vigilance over our spouse, placing ourselves in a parental role. Our spouse, not surprisingly, often began to feel like a naughty, resentful little kid. Others of us withdrew emotionally out of fear of abandonment, driving our spouse further away. These various responses, coming out of our need to control the situation, usually only worsened matters.

In recovery we learn that we cannot control others' behavior. Consequently, there is no need for us to take instant action when they seem headed for disaster. The healthiest thing we can do, both for ourselves and for our relationship, is to detach from the situation and to continue to practice the principles of the program in all aspects of our life. Our commitment to our recovery is the most positive contribution we can make to the survival of the relationship.

If our partners are having a difficult time, they will have to work things out for themselves, with the help of their Higher Power, their own program, and the other people in it. We can be supportive and loving, but we cannot afford to hurl our own recovery out the window in our zeal to make things right. It will not help matters if we allow our spouse's problems to throw us into a relapse.

It may be a different situation, however, if our spouse has another affair or engages in whatever behavior we have decided we cannot live with. In this case, some action by us is clearly needed.

A young woman with a strong religious faith used to believe that marriage was forever, but her recovery program has given her a different perspective. Should her husband, a member of a Twelve Step program for sex addicts, relapse, she has a definite plan that includes calling in outside help (such as church elders), insisting on counseling, and asking for a contract from her husband defining unacceptable behaviors and the consequences for their occurrence. The ultimate consequence, should her husband not be willing to make a real commitment to change, would be the end of the marriage.

It may take a long time in recovery for us to feel free to make a real choice about our marriage. This is why we need to focus on our own recovery. When we are sufficiently healthy, our choices will seem clearer. If our spouse is no longer interested in working a recovery program, we will be able to consider the possibility of leaving the marriage.

For Couples: *What Do We Tell the Rest of the Family, Friends, and People We Work With?*

All addictions involve secrecy. Attempts are made to keep secrets from the spouse, the children, the parents, the neighbors, the employers, and significant others. With sexual addiction, secrecy and shame are even more common than with alcoholism. Many of us spent years denying to ourselves that anything was wrong with our marriage. If we did know about the affairs or other compulsive sexual behavior, we assumed it was somehow our fault. We didn't want other people to know about it because we were sure they would think badly of us if they knew. The sex addict most certainly does not want other family members to know.

Telling the Children

Because addiction affects the whole family, family members should ideally be involved in the recovery process. Most chemical dependency treatment programs do involve the whole family. People in recovery programs for sexual addiction often wonder how much to tell their children. Because of the sensitive nature of sex, a lot depends on the children's ages. Recovering people may choose to talk openly with their teenagers, but to be less explicit with younger children. In families where there is also chemical dependency, some parents emphasize to their children the recovery from alcohol or other drugs and do not discuss the sexual behavior. Where there is no chemical dependency, parents who attend self-help groups and counseling sessions often feel more of a need to explain to the children.

Couples who have shared their problems and their recovery with their teenage or older children have found it beneficial to their relationship with the children and often helpful to the young people in dealing with their own problems. Because of the new information they have, some young adults can recognize their own compulsions and obsessions earlier. They may recognize, for example, that they are using sex compulsively and might seek help years earlier than they otherwise would.

In some families, talking about the addiction may be the first time members have spoken honestly about anything important. Telling the children about the parents' problems also serves to validate the children's own observations. Children usually know a lot more than their parents think. They may overhear arguments and telephone conversations, absorbing information for years and drawing their own conclusions despite their parents' assurances that everything is fine. Discussing the "family secret" with them and allowing them to voice their own impressions about what was happening in the family as they were growing up can validate their perceptions and can correct any misconceptions they may have formed.

Many parents hesitate to talk openly to their children for fear the children will be disillusioned and will withdraw their love and respect.

How one father's openness was helpful to his daughter. . .

When eighteen-year-old Tracy entered into a stormy relationship with a young drug addict, her father decided it was time to talk to her about his past affairs and his involvement in a recovery program. Much to his relief, Tracy did not reject him; on the contrary, she thought it was courageous of him to have told her, and she admired him for the changes that he had been able to make in his life. His story inspired her to get codependency counseling for herself. After some months she was able to break off her relationship with her chemically dependent boyfriend, although she still struggled with feelings of loss. Her father is convinced that his openness with Tracy has been helpful to her.

Of course, telling our children about the past is risky; children do tend to be hurt and angry, and our relationship with them may become strained as a result of what they now know about us. In addition, there is always the risk, when sharing information with children, that they will tell other people who we would prefer not to know. Since there is so much shame associated with compulsive sexual behavior, it is best to wait to talk with our children until we are truly convinced that our addiction or coaddiction is a disease, not a moral failing, and that we can handle the situation if others find out about it.

Covering up the family secret is very much a part of the disease of addiction. It is best that we not share any information with our children if we want them to keep it a secret. Being open with our children is part of *our* recovery; allowing them to share with whomever they want is part of *their* recovery.

A question sometimes asked by spouses in recovery is what we should tell our children if our partner is unwilling to be open with them. (This problem is less likely to occur if both members of the couple are in Twelve Step recovery programs than if only one is in recovery.)

An example of how children usually know a lot more than their parents think...

Joan, forty-four, wanted her children to think well of their father despite his long pattern of affairs and neglect of the marriage. Joan's two children watched silently for years as she went to bed alone crying while their father came home late, smelling of perfume. They noted her pained expressions and her silence as she kept up the appearance that everything was fine. Only after Joan's children left for college and she obtained help for herself did she finally talk with them about her pain.

To her surprise, both children told her they had been aware for years of their father's affairs and simply could not understand her own passivity in the face of such obviously unacceptable behavior. Both revealed their anger at their father and their mixed feelings about her covering up and enabling behaviors. Joan wished she had been more open with her children long ago and had gone to counseling with them to deal with their feelings about their parents.

When Joan was growing up, her parents did not discuss their problems and did not talk about their feelings. She never saw them arguing. Their friends thought Joan had a perfect family, and she grew up believing that pretending to be happy was the normal way to do things.

Joan mistakenly assumed she was protecting her husband's image with the kids. Her children would most likely have grown up healthier had there been more openness between mother and children.

With the increasing acceptance of alcoholism as a disease, it is now possible for a parent to explain to the children that the other parent's uncontrolled drinking and associated behaviors are part of his or her addictive disease. We hope that soon the same acceptance of other addictive behaviors, such as sex addiction and compulsive gambling, as diseases will allow for more open discussion within families when these behaviors are causing problems. Covering up for people's behavior merely protects them from experiencing the consequences of their behavior, delaying the time when they might bottom out and seek treatment. This is as true of sex addiction as it is of alcoholism.

Before we decide to share information about sex addiction and our recovery with our family members, we need to examine our motives for doing so.

- Is it because we want a new level of honesty with those close to us?
- Do we want them to understand what was happening in the family, and to encourage open expression of feelings?
- Or are we inappropriately using our children as confidants, seeking them as allies in our marital struggle?

Telling a child about our spouse's affairs may be a way of

getting back at our partner. The result can be increased disharmony in the family. We may wish to talk with a sponsor and counselor before deciding.

Telling Others

Couples in recovery sometimes need to decide not only what to tell their children, but also what to tell their parents. We often decide to tell them nothing, or very little. But if we feel it is appropriate to share with parents, we might receive information that is helpful in our own recovery. More than one person has been surprised to learn from a parent that the same compulsive behavior was present in the family for several generations.

What to tell business associates is another common problem. One woman said:

"I've tried to separate my professional life and my Twelve Step program. Recently I came back from lunch and was startled to find a telephone message on my office desk which said, 'Please ask your husband to call me to give me information about his Twelve Step program for sex addiction — he's the only local member I know of.' " Her business partners were naturally curious about this organization to which her husband belonged.

As recovering people, Burt and I have tried to keep our professional and personal lives separated. We've both spoken with counselors in our community, telling them about our Twelve Step programs and asking them to have interested people phone us only at home. Nonetheless, on several occasions we have found messages at work similar to the one the woman received. We both finally told our business partners and professional colleagues about our programs. We did not experience any negative consequences. Most people expressed interest and concern.

In workshops we give for counselors and other interested people, we have also shared our recovery experience and have received affirmation from these people for the path we have taken. For Burt, this response has helped lift the shame he felt about past behaviors. Other recovering people also say that acceptance from other people helps them resolve their shame.

On the other hand, it can be a mistake to give out this kind of information, as one man found who told his boss about his program. Shortly thereafter he was fired for what he believed was a trivial reason. He later learned that his employer was himself a practicing sex addict, who reacted very negatively and defensively to the implied labeling of his own behavior as an addiction. The man now believes he was fired because his boss felt too uncomfortable around him after learning about his employee's sex addiction.

The lesson is that we must be extremely careful when sharing our addiction or coaddiction with co-workers. In most circumstances, it may be preferable to keep our personal and professional lives separate. If mentioning that we attend a support group is somehow unavoidable, it may be best to explain only that we are in a recovery program for a problem of a compulsive behavior in the family. Clearly, each situation must be judged individually.

For Couples: *How Can I Talk with Others about My Problems and Recovery Program without Violating My Spouse's Confidentiality?*

"My wife went and told my parents about my addiction..."

"She told them all the ways I'd hurt her and really made me look like the bad guy. She never said a word about any of the crazy stuff *she's* done. She wanted them to believe she was an innocent victim of a terrible person. I felt very angry and betrayed. I did hurt her badly, and I understand she has to talk to people, but it's not fair for her to tell them *my* secrets without also telling her own. Especially my parents." (man, twenty-five, new in recovery; wife not in a recovery program)

"She told people I would never dream of..."

"When my wife first learned about sex addiction and joined a recovery program, she went through an 'evangelical period' where she wanted to let *everyone* know about her discovery.

She told all our friends, including people who I would never dream of sharing such intimate information with. I was very ashamed and embarrassed, and worried about what they might think of *me*. Would they conclude that the problem really was that I was a lousy lover or that she didn't find me attractive enough? I found myself avoiding some of the people she had talked to — and I had the feeling that others were avoiding me." (man, thirty-two, in recovery for three months)

"I find myself ashamed..."

"My wife's friends have noticed she's changing. She has talked with some of them about her S-Anon program [for coaddicts] and how much good it's doing her. But naturally when she talks about being a sexual coaddict she can't help them knowing that her husband is a sex addict! I'd rather some of those people not have that kind of information about me. I know my wife needs to talk with her friends, but, if I know they know, then I find myself ashamed to be around them." (man, fifty, in recovery for four months)

"I don't give out details about his addiction..."

"Part of my recovery is learning how to be more honest and open about my feelings. When I talk with my close friends about my program it naturally involves my husband, but I avoid giving any more information than is necessary in order to explain how *I'm* feeling. I don't give out details about his addiction, only about my own involvement and recovery." (woman, forty, in recovery two years)

Sometimes spouses of alcoholics are unwilling to attend an Al-Anon meeting for fear they will see an acquaintance who will then know that their partner is an alcoholic. They avoid getting help for themselves because they are more concerned about covering up for the addict. In the area of sex addiction, where there is often more shame and secrecy than with alcoholism, this is even a bigger problem. For this reason many spouses of addicts begin getting help for themselves only after their partners get into recovery, or when a counselor suggests they too need a self-help program.

When both of us are in recovery programs, we may feel comfortable talking about ourselves with other members of our group, but we might still have concerns about who else we can confide in. We may worry about tarnishing our spouse's image or we may worry about what our spouse is saying about us. In early recovery, these worries often center on what others will think of us or of our spouse. We usually find that, as our self-esteem improves, these concerns become less important to us. We become more willing to take responsibility for our past actions and learn to trust that our changed life is evidence of the amends we are making for our past behaviors. It becomes less important to us that others see us as perfect people without problems.

Things For the Coaddict to Keep in Mind

We still need to decide what information is appropriate to share about our partner. As one woman put it "It's not okay to share *his* secrets without sharing mine." Information about our partner should be given only if it is relevant to our own recovery. Details about our spouse's present or past behaviors are often best left out of the discussion. If we find ourselves wanting to tell these things to others, we need to examine our motives:

- Do we want to convince our friends we have been victimized?
- Do we want to look like martyrs?
- Are we trying to get back at him or her for some real or imagined hurt?
- Do we want our friends to think less of him or her than they appear to?

Discretion about our partner's sexual behavior is extremely important. There may be legal and social consequences of disclosures we make about our partner's activities. Trusting people with sensitive information is a gamble, as many people have unfortunately learned. We must remember that our focus is on our own recovery. If talking about our program — and therefore giving some information about our partner — is helpful to our recovery, then we become willing to do this, but only with a trusted friend or within the confidential atmosphere of a self-help or therapy group.

Respecting Each Other's Wishes

Some have wondered whether to first get permission before sharing information with others that involves the spouse. This is usually impractical, since the spouse is not often around when we are talking with others. Most of us end up talking about whatever feels comfortable. Nevertheless, many couples agree not to talk about the problem or the program with specific people, without first consulting each other. These "specific people" might include parents and other close relatives, or business associates. Jobs may be jeopardized, and we might not be ready to discuss our sex addiction or coaddiction with our parents — especially parents who sexually molested us as children. At a later stage in our recovery we might be willing to talk with these people, but for now, each spouse needs to respect the other's wishes.

For Couples: *Will Our Sex Life Ever Be Really Good Enough?*

Sex is a particularly important issue in the lives of both members of a couple recovering from the effects of sex addiction. Sex has often been much more than an expression of love for each other. The addict believes it is his or her most important need; the coaddict believes it is the most important sign of love. For both, sex often replaces intimacy. It may be used to forget problems instead of solving them, to temporarily end a serious disagreement that may never get resolved. Some coaddicts have used sex to manipulate — for example, to make sure their partner has a night of "good loving" just before a trip, in the hope they will be less likely to seek another sexual partner while out of town. Consequently, after so many years of ignoring their sexual wishes, some coaddicts may consider sex an unpleasant duty.

Many coaddicts have compared their married life to riding a roller coaster. For some, the uncertainty of their partner's feelings for them and their fear of abandonment were temporarily alleviated only by sex; it was instant reassurance that they were cared for. They also tended to confuse the fear and excitement they felt because of their spouse's unpredictable behavior with the excitement of their lovemaking. Often, after arguing, and then making up by making love, the tension of the argument was experienced as a part of the sexual excitement. Not surprisingly, many coaddicts and addicts considered their lovemaking to be very intense.

When we begin a recovery program, we'll probably initially experience some sexual problems. Some of us were already having problems in this area before recovery; others of us thought that despite our other problems, our sex life was really good. For both types of couples, things may get worse before they get better. Here are some of the problems that couples have shared with us and our thoughts about solutions.

> *"Sex with him during recovery*
> *is less intense than it was before."*
> (female emergency room nurse, thirty-seven)

> *"My wife complains that our sex is less intense. I'm*
> *aware that my high level of sexual energy was a part of my*
> *acting out. Now I can't give her all that sexual energy."*
> (male addictions counselor, thirty-six)

When sex becomes just one of the ways we express our love instead of *the* most important sign of love, when it no longer is enhanced by the fear and excitement of an unstable relationship, it will inevitably appear less intense. Most couples' sexual relationships do change. For people who formerly relied extensively on fantasy during lovemaking and now make love without the fantasies, sex may also feel less intense.

The solution lies in understanding the difference between healthy and unhealthy sexuality. Healthy sexuality may be calmer but also more intimate. The partners are making love to each other instead of just using sex to feel loved or to forget bad feelings.

According to Rosanne, thirty-five:

"I used to do a lot of fantasizing in bed. My body would be making love to my husband, but my mind was miles away with some attractive man who had recently crossed my path. My husband thought I was a terrific lover, but he didn't realize it wasn't *him* I was really making love to. Fantasizing about others may be okay for some people, but not for me. What it did was isolate me from my husband. Now I don't allow myself to fantasize about other men — I want my husband to be the man in my mind as well as in my bed. Now I feel much closer to him emotionally, and I feel a lot better about our lovemaking."

"I feel more inhibited in my lovemaking with my husband than I was before recovery. I'm more aware of what lust is and I'm afraid to provide him with triggers which would get his compulsion started."
(female office worker, twenty-eight)

This young woman feels more restrained and less spontaneous sexually now than when her husband was engaged in compulsive sexual behavior. Her reactions at this stage are natural. Just as spouses of newly-sober alcoholics are often afraid to upset their partners for fear they might resume drinking, she fears that her sexual demands might risk her husband's newfound healthier sexuality. She is still more focused on her spouse's needs than her own. With time, a new balance will be reached and her inhibitions will most likely disappear.

"Before beginning her recovery, my wife never denied me sex. Now she's beginning to assert herself, and I find that I'm afraid to say no to her because maybe she won't give it to me for two weeks after that."
(lawyer, forty-three)

This couple is experiencing a shift in the balance of power in their sexual relationship. Before, the husband made all the decisions about when to have sex. Now they both have a say in it. They are working toward a healthier sexuality, a process that takes time.

53

"Since beginning to work on my sexual addiction, I am impotent with my wife most of the time. I never had this trouble before."
(male computer programmer, thirty-four)

In the past, this young man had frequent sexual relations with prostitutes, whom he perceived as "dirty," whereas his wife was "clean." While having sex with his wife, he used to fantasize about prostitutes. Now that he has banished prostitutes from his life and thoughts, he is unable to have intercourse with his wife. She, meanwhile, is struggling not only to overcome her resentments and health fears over the prostitutes, but also her resentment about the current sexual problems. They are working to develop intimacy in other aspects of their relationship.

This problem is not uncommon. Counseling may help both members of the couple to get through this period in their relationship more comfortably. It may help to know that the situation is usually temporary.

"My husband never asked me before how I felt about various aspects of our lovemaking. Now he wants to know, but I'm embarrassed to talk about it. He also wants me to initiate lovemaking at times, something I've never done before."
(housewife, forty-six)

Many of us were so focused on pleasing our partners that we did not pay attention to our own desires; many of us never learned how to talk with another person about sexual matters. We now need to develop new communication skills in the area of sexuality. Meeting with a third person — such as a counselor or a physician — may make it easier to begin sharing information. We can also experiment with new behaviors, such as initiating lovemaking, even though they may seem strange at first. We can look at this as a wonderful opportunity for us to enhance intimacy in our relationship.

*"My husband no longer wants to go to R-rated movies I'd
like to see and walks out in the middle of some TV programs.
He doesn't want to hear bad language. Our friends think he's
turned into a prude. He's also given up certain sexual activities
we used to do. I don't know what to make of all this."*
(physician's assistant, thirty-eight)

Changes in the sexual relationship with the spouse may be
necessary for a compulsively sexual person. One man, for
example, has identified various triggers that initiate his
fantasizing and addictive thinking. In order to avoid these
triggers, he no longer rents pornographic movies and even
avoids R-rated movies that have scenes of nudity or explicit
lovemaking.

*"My husband is much more interested in sex with me than
he used to be. I liked it better before."*
(businesswoman, forty-one)

This husband used to spend hours with his pornography
collection. He rarely wanted to have sexual relations with his
wife, which was fine with her because she never wanted sex
anyway. She didn't even mind the prostitutes — they kept her
husband occupied so he didn't bother her. Now he's given up
the pornography and the prostitutes and he wants to build
some sexual intimacy with her. This has made her very
uncomfortable, but has made her realize that she too needs
to examine and define her sexuality. She joined a Twelve Step
program and is looking at why she wants to keep her husband
away. Spouses of sex addicts may want to look at their own
sexuality; some may need to examine how they used their
spouse's compulsive sexual behavior to solve their discomfort
with sex. They may want to explore the roots of their attitudes
about sex and, possibly with the help of a counselor, to develop
a more positive, healthier sexuality.

Talking with each other about our feelings is the key to
establishing an improved relationship. Many couples find it
difficult to discuss sex. For those of us who have grown up

believing it's not okay to talk about most feelings, it is especially difficult to talk about our sexual feelings. Twelve Step meetings and counseling sessions are safe places to begin to express feelings such as anger, shame, and confusion. With time, it will become easier to discuss these feelings with our spouse.

Some of us have found that, in recovery, our sexual relationship is better now than ever before. One likely reason is the overall improvement in the rest of our relationship. Another is that sex becomes an affirmation of our commitment to each other, rather than the most important element in our relationship. We feel less isolated, more connected, and more concerned with each other. As the level of trust in each other increases, so does the intimacy and sharing in the marriage.

For Couples: *Getting Beyond Jealousy, Achieving Intimacy, and Enjoying Life*

''He's still out all the time... at self-help meetings...''

"Before recovery, he was out almost every night drinking or with some woman. Now he's *still* out all the time, but I'm not supposed to complain, because he's at self-help meetings. And when he's at home, he's on the telephone a lot. He never used to talk to me much, and now, when he's finally started talking about his feelings, it's not to *me* — his wife — but to strangers." (woman, twenty-eight, new in the recovery program)

''Now that I am in a recovery program and attending meetings...''

"Yes, Helen does attend two meetings daily and spends another hour on the phone, and I do resent it at times, but I know she needs it to stay monogamous. When she was out having affairs we used to have *no* quality time together; any time that we have now is a big improvement. As for me, I used to resent Helen's absences because my life was totally bound up in her. Now that I am in a recovery program and attending meetings myself, I'm working on developing my own interests and activities, and I find I have lots to do while Helen is at a meeting or on the phone. I'm learning to enjoy my alone time." (man, forty, one year in a recovery program)

It is important to remember there can be no recovery for a couple if there is not first individual recovery. Our spouses are doing what is best for them, and, therefore what in the long run will be best for our relationship. Our best approach to dealing with the void we may feel at their continuing absence is to involve ourselves in *our* recovery program: We can attend more meetings, talk with more experienced members about our feelings, and get ourselves sponsors who can share their own experience, strength, and hope. Until we are further along in our own recovery, we will not be ready to work on our marriage

At times, however, feelings of jealousy about the spouse's interactions with others may signal a real problem.

> *''He doesn't talk about his feelings to anyone but his counselor. . .''*

"Richard and I have been in recovery programs for two years, and all that time he has also been seeing a counselor every week. He says she has helped him recognize his feelings and talk about them. The trouble is, he doesn't talk about them to anyone but *her.* Whenever we have a problem or a disagreement, he waits until he's discussed it with her before he's willing to try to resolve it with me. I know she helped him at first, but now he seems more dependent on her than ever. I don't see how Richard and I can ever develop an intimate relationship while she is his confidant."

Richard's counselor may be fostering Richard's dependency on her rather than encouraging him to become independent. His wife is most likely correct in her assessment that they will have difficulty becoming more intimate unless Richard stops using his visits with his counselor for this purpose.

Achieving Intimacy

The relationship of a couple in recovery is not static; as we each proceed separately along our recovery paths, our interactions cannot help but change as well. If we are to succeed as a couple we must be open to these changes and to new ways of relating. In particular, if we previously held on to our spouses as tightly as possible, we must learn to let go and to give them more space. On the other hand, if we spent years avoiding intimacy by fleeing into compulsive sexual behavior, we need to work with our spouse toward more intimacy.

Intimacy, the willingness to let our partner really know us, means exchanging feelings and thoughts in an atmosphere of trust. Intimacy requires vulnerability, the ability to risk being hurt by our partner. People are only willing to be vulnerable if they trust their partner not to take advantage of their vulnerability by hurting them. With the long history coaddicts have of being hurt and disappointed, they may be understandably reluctant to let down their guard and be vulnerable to another person. This is why intimacy is *the* challenge of couples in recovery as well as the goal.

Before there can be true intimacy, there must be trust, which permits the vulnerability that intimacy requires.

Enjoying Life with Friends and Each Other

> *"My fun used to be in pursuing women. Now I don't know how to have fun."*
> (physician, forty-four)

> *"I have no male friends. All my female friends were part of my addiction, so now I have no friends at all."*
> (salesman, thirty-seven)

> *"My husband and I need to find some healthy ways to have excitement in our marriage."*
> (accountant, thirty-five)

Developing intimacy does not always have to be serious business. Having fun together is another means of building a bond between two people. Life does not always have to be serious, and not all activities need to be productive. Many of us who have grown up in unhealthy families have difficulty having fun. This is certainly true of those of us whose energies were previously focused on compulsive sexual behavior or on our spouses.

If it's hard for us to recall the last enjoyable activity we did together, it's time to make some plans. We can go on a picnic, see a movie, play a game of volleyball, take a hike, dig out the old slides and have a slide show, or get up early to watch the sunrise.

We can also begin to develop friendships. A good place to start is with people in our Twelve Step programs, with whom we already share a common language and similar concerns. Going out for coffee after the meeting can be the start of a friendship. Many of us have acquaintances at work who would probably welcome a dinner invitation. When we learn to be friends with other people, we learn to be better friends with our spouse — and with ourselves.

Recovery for couples has unique challenges. But it also provides a wonderful opportunity to make a new start in a relationship with increased intimacy, honesty, and communication. Working through problems together, sharing the experience of spiritual growth in a Twelve Step program, learning to communicate in the language of the recovery program, making new friends who are also in recovery — all these shared experiences can create a powerful bond between partners, giving them a better relationship than they ever had before. Furthermore, through recovery, they will each be in the marriage by choice and not because they need another person in order to feel whole.

In our own relationship, we acknowledge that we are with each other by choice, one day at a time. It's not always easy, and there have been times we have felt like giving up. We each would be okay without the other, but we would miss the special joys of being together. As we have grown in our programs in the past five years, we have experienced a new serenity and intimacy that we never thought possible. Our trust in each other is far stronger than before we began our recovery. We are closer than ever before and, as best friends, we look forward to continuing our journey together. For us, the struggles have been well worth the rewards. We wish the same for you.

APPENDIX A

*The Twelve Steps of Alcoholics Anonymous**

1. We admitted we were powerless over alcohol—that our lives had become unmanageable.
2. Came to believe that a Power greater than ourselves could restore us to sanity.
3. Made a decision to turn our will and our lives over to the care of God *as we understood Him.*
4. Made a searching and fearless moral inventory of ourselves.
5. Admitted to God, to ourselves, and to another human being the exact nature of our wrongs.
6. Were entirely ready to have God remove all these defects of character.
7. Humbly asked Him to remove our shortcomings.
8. Made a list of all persons we had harmed, and became willing to make amends to them all.
9. Made direct amends to such people wherever possible, except when to do so would injure them or others.
10. Continued to take personal inventory and when we were wrong promptly admitted it.
11. Sought through prayer and meditation to improve our conscious contact with God *as we understood Him,* praying only for knowledge of His will for us and the power to carry that out.
12. Having had a spiritual awakening as the result of these steps, we tried to carry this message to alcoholics, and to practice these principles in all our affairs.

---

*The Twelve Steps of A.A. are taken from *Alcoholics Anonymous* (Third Edition), published by A.A. World Services, Inc., New York, N.Y., 59-60. Reprinted with permission.

APPENDIX B

Resources

Sexaholics Anonymous (*for sex addicts*)
General Services Office
Box 300
Simi Valley, CA 93062

S-Anon (*for families of sex addicts*)
P.O. Box 5117
Sherman Oaks, CA 91413

Twin Cities Sex Addicts Anonymous (*for sex addicts*)
P.O. Box 3038
Minneapolis, MN 55403

Twin Cities Co-S.A. (*for families of sex addicts*)
P.O. Box 14537
Minneapolis, MN 55414

Sex and Love Addicts Anonymous (*for sexual addicts*)
P.O. Box 88, New Town Branch
Boston, MA 02258

APPENDIX C
Suggested Reading

Beattie, Melody. *Codependent No More*. Center City, Minn.: Hazelden Educational Materials, 1986.

Brown, Gabrielle. *The New Celibacy*. New York: Ballantine Books, 1980.

Carnes, Patrick. *Out of the Shadows: Understanding Sexual Addiction*. Minneapolis, Minn.: CompCare, 1983.

Dobson, James C. *Love Must be Tough*. Waco, Tex.: Word Publishing, 1983.

Halpern, Howard. *How to Break Your Addiction to a Person*. New York: Bantam Books, 1981.

Hope and Recovery: A Twelve Step Guide for Healing from Compulsive Sexual Behavior. Minneapolis, Minn.: CompCare, 1987.

Larsen, Earnie. *Stage II Recovery*. San Francisco: Harper & Row, 1985.

Larsen, Earnie. *Stage II Relationships*. San Francisco: Harper & Row, 1987.

Maxwell, Ruth. *The Booze Battle*. New York: Ballantine Books, 1976.

Norwood, Robin. *Women Who Love Too Much*. Los Angeles: Jeremy Tarcher, Inc., 1985.

Norwood, Robin. *Letters from Women Who Love Too Much*. New York: Pocket Books, 1988.

Schneider, Jennifer. *Back from Betrayal: Recovering from His Affairs*. Center City, Minn.: Hazelden Educational Materials, 1988.

Sexaholics Anonymous. Simi Valley, Calif.: Sexaholics Anonymous, 1984.

Smedes, Lewis. *Forgive and Forget*. New York: Pocket Books, 1984.

Other titles that will interest you...

Back from Betrayal
Recovering from His Affairs
by Jennifer P. Schneider, M.D.
If your man's affairs have made your life unmanageable, this book was written for you. Here is guidance to help you understand and change your behavior. You'll begin to realize why you are obsessed with him, why you try to control him, why you stay with a man who is unfaithful. *Back from Betrayal* will help you to an awareness that your most important responsibility is to yourself. Hardcover, 256 pp.
Order No. 5032

Codependent No More
by Melody Beattie
The definitive book about codependency, *Codependent No More* is for everyone who has suffered the torment of loving too much. Melody Beattie explains what codependency is, what it isn't, who's got it, and how to move beyond it. This book will be a boon to your self-esteem. 208 pp.
Order No. 5014

Is It Love or Is It Addiction?
by Brenda Schaeffer
This dynamic book helps us understand love addiction, how and why we fall into it, how to identify it, and how to get out of it. Step-by-step, Brenda Schaeffer helps us sort out the unhealthy, addictive elements in our relationships. 158 pp.
Order No. 5022
